GOD LOVES ME AND I LOVE ME TOO!

NEW SEED INDUSTRIES ©
Create. Grow. Disperse.
(A Christian Publishing Company)

Published by New Seed Industries, LLC
West Bloomfield, MI   Email: newseedllc@gmail.com
www.newseedindustries.com

God Loves Me and I Love Me Too!
ISBN-13: 978-1-7369277-3-1

Printed in the U.S.A

WRITTEN BY: TIFANIE GOODMAN

COVER DESIGN BY ROBERT COLES

ILLUSTRATED BY: ROBERT COLES

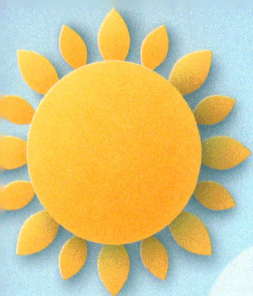

DO YOU KNOW WHO GOD MADE ME?

GOD MADE ME GREAT.

**THANK YOU GOD
THAT I AM GREAT.**

GOD MADE ME BRAVE.

THANK YOU GOD
THAT I AM BRAVE.

GOD GIVES ME PEACE.

THANK YOU GOD
THAT I HAVE PEACE.

GOD MADE ME CREATIVE.

THANK YOU GOD
I AM CREATIVE.

GOD GIVES ME JOY.

THANK YOU GOD
THAT I HAVE JOY.

GOD MADE ME GOOD.

THANK YOU GOD
THAT I AM GOOD.

GOD MADE ME CONFIDENT.

**THANK YOU GOD
THAT I AM CONFIDENT.**

GOD MADE ME A LEADER.

THANK YOU GOD
THAT I AM A LEADER.

GOD MADE ME WONDERFUL.

THANK YOU GOD
I AM WONDERFUL.

GOD MADE ME SPECIAL.

**THANK YOU GOD
THAT I AM SPECIAL.**

GOD MADE ME.

GOD LOVES ME.

I KNOW WHO GOD MADE ME.

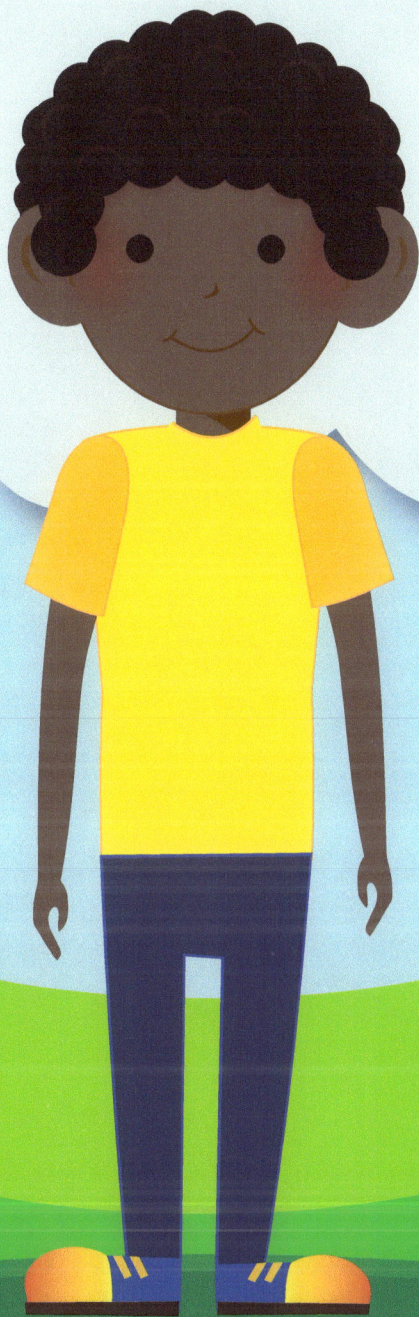

AND I LOVE ME TOO!

DAILY PRAYER

I AM THE HEAD AND NOT THE TAIL.
I AM ABOVE AND NOT BENEATH.
I AM THE GIVER AND NOT THE BORROWER.
I AM THE LEADER AND NOT THE FOLLOWER.
I AM COVERED BY THE BLOOD OF JESUS.
AMEN.